Americans All biographies are inspiring life stories about people of all races, creeds, and nationalities who have uniquely contributed to the American way of life. Highlights from each person's story develop his contributions in his special field — whether they be in the arts, industry, human rights, education, science and medicine, or sports.

Specific abilities, character, and accomplishments are emphasized. Often despite great odds, these famous people have attained success in their fields through the good use of ability, determination, and hard work. These fast-moving stories of real people will show the way to better understanding of the ingredients necessary for personal success.

Walter Reed

PIONEER IN MEDICINE

by Lynn Groh

illustrated by Frank Vaughn

GARRARD PUBLISHING COMPANY

CHAMPAIGN, ILLINOIS

Especially for Ellen

Picture credits:

National Library of Medicine, Bethesda, Md.: p. 2, 36, 62, 81, 85, 87, 90

Contents

1. The Scars of War

Thirteen-year-old Walter Reed lay very still and tried not to think about food. His supper of corn bread and buttermilk had been filling, but he knew that soon he would feel hungry again. The Civil War had been in progress for four years, and no Southerner had enough to eat.

"Go to sleep quickly, then it won't seem so long until breakfast," his older brother Chris said from the other side of the big four-poster bed that the boys shared.

No sooner had he drifted off to sleep than Walter was suddenly awakened by a strong hand gently shaking his shoulder.

He opened his eyes, blinking in the soft glow of a candle held by his father. He did not have to ask what was wrong when he saw the expression on Pa's face.

"Union raiders are coming!" Walter exclaimed, leaping to the floor as Chris tumbled out of the other side of the bed.

"Yes. A farmer saw them making camp about fifteen miles from town," Pa said quickly. "He's spreading the word. Joey Rogers came over from his farm, and he's waiting to help you hide the horses."

The raiders were soldiers of the Union army who searched the countryside for supplies. They especially wanted horses for the cavalry to ride, but they also took food and anything else of value.

Walter and Chris found Ma in the kitchen, storing food in big pots that Pa would bury in the garden. Their sister

Laura was tying the silver candlesticks and table silver in bundles to be dropped into the well. When the soldiers came, Pa would tell them that other raiders had been there and had taken everything.

"Be careful," Ma said anxiously, as she handed Walter a basket of food.

"We'll send for you when the raiders leave," Pa said. "If you run out of food, one of you come back after dark to get more."

Joey and a young farmhand named Jeff, who worked on the Rogers' farm nearby, were waiting at the stable on the Rogers' two horses. Walter and Chris mounted Turnip and Bess, the only horses Pa had left, and the four boys galloped off through the dark to the Meherrin River, just outside the small town of Lawrenceville, Virginia.

Joey, the oldest, led the way along the riverbank. They moved slowly in single file, letting the horses find their own way through a thick growth of scrubby trees and underbrush. Bushes tore at their legs. Wet, hanging vines slapped at their faces.

Jeff was so afraid of the dark that he kept begging Joey to let him go home. He started at every night noise he heard,

and Walter tried to reassure his frightened companion.

"No one is there, Jeff," Walter kept saying. "It's only frogs and insects."

It was after midnight when Joey finally found a spot he thought was safe enough for them to use as a hiding place—a clearing in a dense thicket at the edge of a swamp. The weary boys staked the horses, then wrapped themselves in the saddle blankets. With their saddles for pillows, they lay down to sleep.

When Walter awoke the next morning, there was no head on the saddle next to his own. Jeff was gone.

"Maybe he went to get more food," Walter suggested.

"Not in broad daylight!" Joey said angrily. "The raiders might see him. He'll give away our hiding place."

The boys tried to keep busy in order to pass the time. It seemed like a very long day. Darkness came, but Jeff did not return, and there was still no sign of him the next morning. The boys decided to go to the river to bathe. They were gone only a short time, but when they returned to their campsite a reception committee awaited them—a band of Yankee soldiers.

To Walter's surprise the Yankees did not look fierce at all. They only looked tired and worn-out in their rumpled blue uniforms. They were just young men, like Walter's own brothers, Jim and Tom, who were away fighting with the Confederate army.

The lieutenant who was in charge of the raiders spoke sternly, but there was a hint of laughter in his eyes as he looked at the three young Rebels. "You hid well," he said. "We would never have found you without your friend's help. We saw him on the road yesterday. He was covered with mud, so we guessed he had been at the river. He was so frightened when we stopped him that he told us your hiding place even before we asked."

The lieutenant said he would have to take the boys to the raiders' camp. "We can't let you go to warn everyone else that we are here."

The boys knew better than to tell him that everyone already knew. That would only cause the Yankees to search houses more closely for hidden valuables.

The raiders held the boys for only a short time. They broke camp the next morning, and the lieutenant told the young prisoners to go home. The Yankees took the four horses, however.

Walter could be brave about being a prisoner, but how could he ever face his father? Pa had trusted him to save the horses, and he had failed.

Ma and Pa could not keep back the tears of relief when their sons reached home safely. "But they took Bess and Turnip!" Walter sobbed, forgetting that thirteen was too old for crying.

14

"Silly boy! *You* are safe," Pa exclaimed. "We can get along without the horses."

About a week later the news reached Lawrenceville that General Robert E. Lee had surrendered the Confederate army on April 9, 1865. The war was over. Soon Walter's brother Tom came home, safe and well. Later the oldest brother, Jim, arrived, but the left sleeve of his coat was empty. His arm had been shot away by a cannon ball.

"The war has left scars, but we must let them heal," Pa said. "Don't waste time in bitterness over past events. Prepare yourselves to be useful men in the future."

Mr. Reed was a Methodist circuit rider. He was a minister who served not one church, but several churches located in rural communities scattered about in one area of the state. Every two years the

16

church leaders sent Mr. Reed to a new circuit. Pa always went willingly wherever he was sent, and he had never asked a special favor.

In the fall of 1865, however, Mr. Reed appealed to the church leaders to send him to Charlottesville, where there was a university. He hoped they might allow him to remain there long enough for his sons to finish college. The church leaders agreed.

"Ma and I will manage somehow to give you an education," Pa told his sons. "Only you can decide what kind of men you will be."

2. No Time for Rules

The autumn night was warm and the big parlor in the Methodist parsonage in Charlottesville was quiet, although the entire Reed family was gathered there. The light from the oil lamp seemed to grow dimmer and Walter began to nod over his Greek grammar. He shook his head to arouse himself and started to get up to open a window.

At that moment Ma, who sat sewing in a big chair near the fireplace, began to cough. She tried to stifle the sound with her handkerchief, but everyone heard her. Walter sat down again. The windows had to be kept closed because night air was bad for Ma's asthma.

Pa's quill pen stopped moving across the page, but he did not look up from the sermon he was busy preparing. Laura looked anxiously at her mother, then quickly bent over her sewing again. The four boys pretended to be absorbed in their school books, even though they cast secret, worried glances toward their sick mother. No one spoke. Ma did not like for the family to make a fuss about her illness.

"I'll be all right—just as soon as spring comes again and I can start working in my flower garden," she insisted.

"This time we are going to stay here long enough for you to enjoy your own flowers," Pa said, trying to make his voice sound cheerful.

As fall turned into winter, however, Ma rested in bed more and more often, and Laura woke up early to prepare school lunches for the boys. Walter and Chris then started out to attend Charlottesville Institute, a boys' school that was similar to a modern high school. Jim and Tom walked in the opposite direction, to the University of Virginia.

After school, the boys had time for only a few chores before dinner, which was followed by three or four hours of study. Ma and Laura spent those hours mending shirts and making over dresses to save money for the boys' education. Virginia had no public schools at that time, so Pa paid tuition for Walter and Chris at Charlottesville Institute as well as for Jim and Tom at the University of Virginia.

Walter was very concerned about the sacrifices his parents and Laura made so that the boys could go to school. Since he was the youngest, Pa would still be paying tuition for him when the older boys had found jobs. And Walter could not even decide what he wanted to be. Jim was studying theology so that he could become a minister like his father. Tom had decided to be a lawyer, and Chris also planned to study law when he entered the university the next year.

"I want to do something to help people, like Pa does—but I don't know what," Walter said.

"You have lots of time to decide what you will be. For now, your job is to learn your lessons well," Ma said kindly.

22

In February 1866, Ma became too ill to leave her bed. Probably her asthma was complicated by some other ailment. Doctors of that time did not know about virus infections or respiratory diseases, and there were no medicines to treat such diseases. People believed that diseases were caused by night air and "miasma," a poisonous vapor that was supposed to rise up from the earth. The known "remedies" for Mrs. Reed's illness were hot foot-baths, hot mustard plasters applied to the chest to ease coughing, and cold baths to reduce fever. But these remedies did not help Ma, and she died.

For a time Walter was so sad he did not want to study, or even go to school. He also worried about Laura, who now had to manage the household alone.

"Laura shouldn't have to take care of

me—I'm almost grown," Walter said to Chris. "I'm going to finish my education in a hurry."

In those days students were not required to attend the institute for a certain number of years. They were graduated as soon as they could pass an extremely difficult examination, covering all the subjects taught. Walter studied constantly, determined to graduate in record time. With extra help from his headmaster, William Richardson Abbot, Walter was ready for the school's big examination at the end of his second year. Most students took three or four years to prepare for the exam.

Walter passed and was graduated with honors from the institute. Now he was ready to enter the University of Virginia. Much to his disappointment the university

24

officials said Walter was too young. He would be only sixteen years old when the fall term began. The age of entering students was usually about seventeen or eighteen.

Walter could not wait a whole year! Mr. Abbot called on the officials and showed them Walter's high marks. He told them that Walter was more grown-up than many older boys. The officials finally agreed to set aside the rules this one time, and Walter began his studies that fall— the youngest student to enter the university since its founding many years before.

Walter upset another of the university rules. At the end of his first year, he asked permission to take the final examination and receive his degree. This time the answer was no. Sixteen was too young even to be in college—it was certainly too young to graduate. Soon Walter went back to the officials with another idea. Since he had to stay another year, he wanted to study something useful. "If I can pass the medical exam, will you give me a doctor's degree at the end of the year?" he asked.

The officials were astonished. No one had ever completed the medical course in one year. They decided to teach this ambitious young man a lesson. Certainly, they told him, smiling knowingly at one another. He would receive the degree in medicine at the end of the college year— if he passed the examination.

It was Walter who smiled last. He did pass the examination at the end of the year, and he was graduated third highest in his class. He was the youngest ever to receive that degree from the university.

The entire Reed family attended the
graduation ceremony—and it was a much
larger family now. Jim, who was now a
circuit rider, brought his new wife. Tom
and Chris, both lawyers, were there with
Laura, who was engaged to be married.
Pa had remarried, and Walter had a little
half sister named Annie. At last he was
no longer the baby of the family. From

that day on, the preacher's youngest son would be known as Dr. Walter Reed.

Pa thought an honor student should have the best of training, and that fall, when he himself went back to riding the circuits, he managed to scrape up enough money to send Walter and Chris to New York City. There Walter planned to take advanced medical training at the famous Bellevue Hospital, while Chris took some graduate law courses at Columbia University. They hoped to find jobs to pay their expenses.

Walter knew he could never repay his father, but he resolved that Pa would have reason to be proud of his youngest son.

3. Love Finds a Way

Rain beat against the windows of the small Brooklyn apartment that Walter shared with Chris. The sound was as doleful as Walter's spirits at the moment.

"What do you think Pa would say if I quit medicine?" he asked suddenly.

Chris could only stare at his brother in disbelief. "You can't mean that!" he finally said. "You can't throw away all your years of study and work."

"Don't get so excited," Walter smiled. "I won't quit medicine, but I would like to quit New York."

"I thought you liked it here, and you're doing just great in your work," Chris said.

Walter *had* been thrilled by the bustling activity of the fabulous city of one million people. He could still remember the excitement of his two years of study at Bellevue Hospital and his year as an intern at Kings County Hospital in Brooklyn. Walter's work had attracted the attention of Dr. Joseph C. Hutchison, a famous New York surgeon who was also a member of the Board of Health. When Walter received his medical license, Dr. Hutchison gave him a job as a health inspector—a position much like that of a Public Health Service doctor today.

The salary was low, but it was enough to support Walter. He and Chris, who had joined a New York law firm after graduating from Columbia University, lived modestly and shared expenses. "But I can't support a family on my salary," he said hopelessly.

"So that's what's wrong with you— you're in love!" Chris teased.

Walter smiled shyly. He had fallen in love with a young girl, Emilie Lawrence, while visiting his family in Murfreesboro, North Carolina. Pa had recently been sent there by the church. Walter had known her only a short time, but he knew Emilie was the girl he wanted to marry. He could not ask her to become his wife, however, until he was earning enough to support a family.

Walter could earn more money by building a private practice as a doctor. However, he worked long hours at his job each day and had little time left to care for patients of his own.

"New York is too big and too heartless," he explained. "Day after day I treat sick people who need only a clean place in which to live and enough good food to eat. No one cares, and I can't really help these people. I would like to live in a small city where I would not feel so helpless and lost."

Walter did not have enough money to open an office and wait for patients to come to him. "I might have to take a job in some other field in order to earn enough money to set up my own practice," he said.

A few days later, Walter read in a newspaper that the Army Medical Corps would soon hold an examination to select doctors to serve in the army. A sudden thought occurred to him! If he served for three or four years in the army, he could save enough money to start a private practice. He decided to take the test.

"I'll really have to cram—the exam will cover everything, even Greek and history!" he told Chris. "I've been out of school too long to remember those subjects."

In the weeks before the examination, Walter hurried home after each day's work and studied far into the night. Chris began to worry about his brother's health. Then finally, on February 5, 1875, Walter reported for the examination. His heart sank. The army needed only 30 doctors but 500 men took the examination. It lasted five hours a day for six days. When the grades were announced, Walter was thrilled to find that he was one of the 30 doctors chosen. He was assigned to Willetts Point, an army post on Long Island.

Walter hurried to Murfreesboro to ask Emilie to marry him. Emilie accepted, and they set their wedding date for June of 1876. Walter reported happily to his first post, only to learn that his orders had been changed. He would remain only a few months at Willetts Point. On the day

Walter Reed began his lifelong career with the army as a young medical corps doctor.

set for his wedding he would be on his way to a post in Arizona. Walter had always wanted to see the West—but not now!

Only a few weeks before he was to go West, Walter was given a leave to visit his family. Sadly he went to Murfreesboro to say good-bye to Emilie. He could not ask her to leave her comfortable home for the hardships of life on the western frontier. The wedding would have to wait until he returned.

Emilie insisted that she, too, had always wanted to see the West, and that life on the frontier would be a great adventure. Walter was too happy to argue, and they were married on April 25. Emilie stayed behind when Walter left for Arizona. She would follow in the fall when the weather was cooler.

In June Walter first escorted a group of soldiers west from New York to San Francisco, then traveled alone to his post in Arizona. There was great excitement among the young recruits who were going west for the first time. As the journey began, the eastern newspapers were filled with accounts of the army's battles with the Sioux Indians who, led by Chiefs Sitting Bull and Crazy Horse, were on the warpath. The army was massing troops for a final battle to force the Sioux onto a reservation.

Most of the soldiers' ideas about the West came from tall tales of daring adventure told by "Buffalo Bill" Cody. He was the Indian scout, buffalo hunter, and pony express rider who had become an entertainer, putting on his "Wild West Show" in the East. For many of these soldiers, however, the eight-day journey by train across the continent was a disappointment.

The romantic stories told about the Great Plains did not come to life for the soldiers. The plains proved to be flat, barren, and almost unbearably hot. As seen from the windows of the rickety wooden passenger car, the majestic Rocky Mountains were sheer, unfriendly walls of rock. The travelers did not see one Indian in war dress. Their train crossed southern Wyoming, while the Sioux were on the warpath in Montana, many miles to the north.

Walter, however, was awed by the vastness of his country and its prairies, mountains, rivers, and forests. He went by steamboat from San Francisco down the coast of California to San Diego.

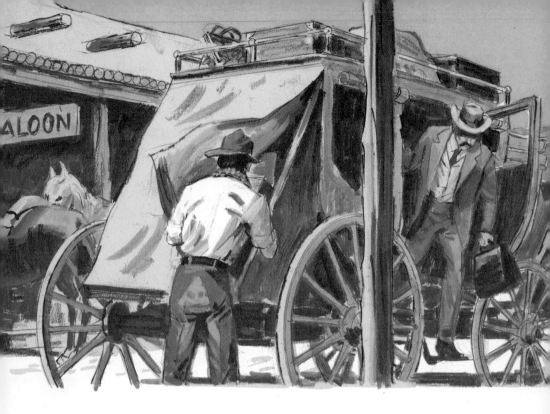

Then he still had a difficult journey by
stagecoach, across southern California and
the coastal range to Fort Yuma in
Arizona. The temperature rarely dropped
below 115 degrees at this fort which was
reputed to be the hottest of all army
posts. Walter stayed here for two months
and then received orders for Fort Lowell
near Tucson, Arizona.

He was dismayed when he reached this

little Spanish-speaking town. One street with a general store and many saloons was all there was. Fort Lowell, where he was stationed, was a cluster of wooden barracks and a few officers' adobe dwellings huddled in the vast, empty desert. It was the loneliest place Walter had ever seen.

What kind of life would this be for Emilie?

4. Wild West Doctor

Emilie turned in the doorway to take one last look at the little four-room adobe house that had been her home for eight months. At that moment her little dog Undina set up a fierce barking, its tiny body stiff with fury.

Emilie knew what that meant—their good friend the post chaplain had come to say good-bye to Walter and Emilie who were leaving Fort Lowell. The chaplain had with him his pet gila monster, Undina's enemy.

"Too bad they never became friends," Emilie said, as Walter swept the dog up in his arms to stop its barking.

"Too bad Sally Anne is not civilized enough to come out of her cage to say good-bye properly," the chaplain said. He looked reproachfully at the scaly, black and orange desert lizard which crouched in its wooden cage, its tongue flicking angrily at the dog. "I still have hopes of teaching her some manners."

Emilie doubted that the deadly gila monster could be tamed, but she understood the chaplain's attachment to it. "That is one lesson the desert has to teach," she said. "There is so little life here that one learns to cherish each living thing."

"It will be even lonelier at Camp Apache," the chaplain warned. "Here at least we have the stagecoach twice a month and a cattle driver drifting by from time to time. But nothing ever happens at Camp Apache."

"I hope nothing happens, since the Apache Indians will be our neighbors," Walter said.

A year earlier, Colonel Custer and all his men had been massacred at the Little Bighorn in Wyoming by Sioux warriors led by Crazy Horse and Sitting Bull. Western settlers had feared that other tribes would go on the warpath. The Apaches, however, had remained peacefully on their reservation in the White Mountains north of Tucson. The Reeds had no fear of the Indians as they set out for Camp Apache, which was near the reservation.

To reach their new post the Reeds

traveled by army wagon across a rugged mountain range, through passes so rough that horses got through only with difficulty. In many places, the soldiers who escorted the Reeds had to lift the wagons over boulders or lower them with ropes down steep cliffs. Beyond the mountain range there was not even a tiny village— only Camp Apache and the reservation. Few people traveled there except army couriers and those driving supply wagons.

The Reeds were scarcely settled in their log cabin when a son, Walter Lawrence Reed, was born on December 4, 1877. They called him Lawrence in honor of his mother's family. There were no nurses or servants at Camp Apache. Dr. Reed was nursemaid, cook, and housekeeper until Emilie was able to take charge again.

Lawrence was only about four months

old when peaceful Camp Apache had an Indian alarm. A rancher rode into the fort to report that Apaches had not only raided his ranch but also several others.

These Indians, led by the outlaw chief Geronimo, had escaped from their reservation. Soldiers from Camp Apache were sent to capture them.

One night Dr. Reed was awakened by a loud pounding on his door. He opened it to find two big, awkward soldiers. In his arms one of them was holding a little Indian girl, five or six years old.

"We came upon Geronimo's camp," the soldier explained. "All of the Apaches got away, except for this little girl. She tried to run, but she fell into the campfire and was left behind."

Dr. Reed took the little girl to the infirmary. He stayed by her bedside for

hours, treating her burns. He saved her life, but no one knew where to return the little girl because her people were hiding.

"We will just have to keep her," Emilie said firmly. The Reeds named the little girl Susie and raised her as their own.

"Our friend the chaplain told us that nothing ever happens at Camp Apache!" Walter said.

Walter and Emilie had seen quite enough of the "Wild West," however, and they were overjoyed when another doctor arrived to replace Walter. In the spring of 1880, the Reed household—Walter, Emilie, Lawrence, Susie, and the little dog Undina—went East.

"Back to civilization!" Emilie said with relief.

The Reeds were soon reminded, however, that civilization has its problems, too.

5. The "Invisible World"

A mounted policeman galloped up to the army barracks in Washington, D. C. He leaped from his horse and rushed breathlessly into headquarters.

"President Garfield has been shot!" he exclaimed to the officer on duty. "We caught the assassin, but the army will have to take charge."

The officer ordered a company of military policemen to the scene. "You'd better go with them, Captain Reed," he said to Walter. "A doctor might be needed."

For several hours, Dr. Reed stood guard over the man, clearly deranged, who had shot President James A. Garfield as he was preparing to board a train at the Washington railroad station on July 2, 1881. The president was not killed instantly. For two months, doctors tried desperately to save his life, but the wound was too severe and President Garfield died in September.

Walter was deeply saddened by the tragic event. He had been depressed ever since his return to "civilization" a year earlier. While he was in the West, great new medical discoveries, made by scientists in Europe, had been introduced in American medical schools. Walter heard the younger doctors and medical students talking of an invisible world of germs, which man can see only with the aid of a microscope. They spent much of their time in laboratories, poring over microscopes and test tubes.

These germs, or bacteria, caused diseases, Dr. Reed's colleagues told him. The old theories that disease was caused by filth, night air, and the mysterious vapor called "miasma" had now been discarded. Modern doctors studied bacteriology to learn how to cure diseases by destroying the bacteria that caused them.

Dr. Reed was eager to study this new branch of medicine. However, with a family to support, he could not afford to return to medical school. "I will have to teach myself," he said to Emilie. "I will stay in the army so you and the children will be secure while I study bacteriology."

Dr. Reed had no laboratory. Many people did not believe that bacteria cause disease, and Congress would not provide money to build laboratories in army hospitals. Dr. Reed had to be content with reading about the tiny germs that other scientists saw under their microscopes. He collected all of the medical journals and reports he could find, and studied them carefully.

It was the custom for army officers to be moved to a new post about every two years. In 1882, after two years in the East, Dr. Reed was sent to still another frontier post, Fort Omaha, near the town of Omaha in the northwest prairie country of Nebraska. Later the Reeds moved on to Fort Sidney, then to Fort Robinson, and each new post was lonelier than the one before. Only an occasional homesteader's sod shanty appeared on the vast, rolling plains. In summer the grasslands, dried by drought and blazing sun, were swept by prairie fires. In winter, raging blizzards and snowstorms buried homes and livestock, and blocked roads for weeks at a time.

On the lonely frontier, Dr. Reed had no other scientists to talk to, and there were no hospitals where he might go for help with his studies. The army outposts had no schools even for Lawrence, and the Reeds had to send their young son away to a boarding school in Virginia. They now had a little girl, born July 12, 1883. She was named Emilie Lawrence Reed, for her mother, but the Reeds called her Blossom. Even with Susie and Blossom to care for, Emilie still missed her son.

Dr. Reed spent long, snowbound evenings studying medical journals which he had ordered from the East and from

Europe. He taught himself to read German and Italian so that he could study the reports which European scientists made. Reading about bacteria and viruses was not enough, Dr. Reed realized. He knew he must have a laboratory in which to experiment for himself.

"Perhaps you will be sent to a post in the East, close to a hospital that has a laboratory," Emilie said hopefully.

Instead, the Reeds went from Nebraska to Mount Vernon Barracks near Mobile, Alabama. Like his father before him, Dr. Reed hated to ask special favors from his superiors, but his yearning to learn more about medicine was too strong. At the end of his assignment in Alabama, he asked to be sent to Baltimore, Maryland, and to be allowed to take courses at Johns Hopkins Hospital. He got the post.

In October 1890, thirty-nine-year-old Walter Reed became a student again. In the laboratory at Johns Hopkins, he at last was able to see the tiny organisms about which he had been reading, and to study their habits. Under his microscope the world of bacteria was no longer invisible.

At first Walter worked with doctors who served as instructors at the hospital, but soon he began special studies of his own. His fellow doctors considered Dr. Reed an outstanding bacteriologist.

At the end of the year, Dr. Reed was ordered to Fort Snelling in Minnesota, another frontier post. Before leaving, he asked the army for money to set up a small laboratory to continue his medical research. The surgeon general was one of those who did not believe in the "invisible world." He refused Dr. Reed's request.

In his bitter disappointment, Walter at first felt that he had been betrayed by the army he had served so long. He was a soldier, however, and he was his father's son. The soldiers at Fort Snelling must have a doctor. Walter Reed had been chosen for the job, and he would go.

6. A Dream Comes True

"I have found a laboratory!"

Dr. Reed's voice was jubilant as he burst in upon his family with his happy announcement. Emilie looked up from her sewing, and a smile lit up her face.

"Why, that's wonderful!" she said. "Now everything is perfect."

The Reeds had stayed at Fort Snelling only a few months before moving to St. Paul, Minnesota. St. Paul was a small town then, but it offered a more comfortable home for Emilie, and there were

good schools so that Lawrence could be with the family again. Now, at last, Dr. Reed could return to the research he had longed to do.

The laboratory was only a very crude arrangement set up by a young biology teacher, Louis Wilson, at the local high school. He had assembled tables, a few test tubes, a microscope, and a gas range which he borrowed from the homemaking department.

"You can share my laboratory—if you will teach me bacteriology," the eager young scientist told Dr. Reed.

Dr. Reed was happy to teach what he knew about bacteriology to anyone who would learn, and he found young Louis a diligent student. He also made a new discovery about himself—he liked teaching.

The two new friends chose an ambitious

project—the study of the bacterium that causes diphtheria. They hoped to find a way to protect people against it. Doctors of the area provided specimens, or samples, of this bacterium, obtained by swabbing with cotton the throats of their diphtheria patients. The cotton swabs were packed in special test tubes and sent to Dr. Reed and Louis for study.

Dr. Reed's dream of a fine laboratory became a reality at the Army Medical School.

Just as the study began, Dr. Reed was ordered to move again—to the new Army Medical School in Washington, D. C. The former surgeon general had retired and had been succeeded by Dr. George Miller Sternberg, who believed in research.

Dr. Sternberg, a friend of Walter's for many years, knew of his work in bacteriology. The doctors who had instructed Walter at Johns Hopkins Hospital recommended him highly. Dr. Sternberg chose Dr. Reed to be one of the professors at his new Army Medical School.

The wandering Reeds finally settled into a permanent home in the nation's capital. In addition to teaching courses in bacteriology, Dr. Reed also served as curator, or director, of the school's medical museum. This was an enormous laboratory with materials for medical research.

Dr. Reed spent many hours at the museum, helping students and also doing research of his own. Whenever new bacteria were discovered, he obtained specimens to grow in his own laboratory. He patiently studied each one to learn its life history, how it reproduced, how it traveled from one place to another, and what effect it had on people. He described his studies in papers he wrote for medical journals.

For Dr. Reed this was the perfect life. "I miss working with patients," he confessed to Emilie. "Still, by teaching other doctors, I'm helping a great many more patients. Ten new doctors will treat ten times as many patients as I would."

But life did not remain so ideal. In 1898, the United States went to war. Angry feelings had been growing between the United States and Spain for some time. On February 15, 1898, the American battleship *Maine* was blown up in Havana harbor in Cuba, then a Spanish possession. The Americans accused the Spanish of destroying the ship, and on April 25 the United States declared war against Spain.

Sorrowfully Walter Reed watched in Washington as thousands of young Americans rushed to take part in the Spanish-American war. His son, Lawrence, now twenty years old, was among them. Walter Reed knew well the horrors of war from the Civil War of his childhood. But the doctor also knew that a greater horror awaited these young men: disease.

"In every major war throughout history, more soldiers have died of disease than have been killed in battle," Dr. Reed said to Emilie. "I fear that this war will not be different." His fears proved correct. The war was over within four months— but American soldiers continued to die by the hundreds in army camps in their own country. The killer was one of the "fevers," but camp officials could not agree on which fever was to blame. All efforts to control the epidemic had failed.

Surgeon General Sternberg knew just the man to solve the problem. He sent Walter Reed to tour the army camps and to investigate the problem.

7. Tracking the Invisible Killers

The first disease-stricken army post Dr. Reed visited was Camp Alger in Virginia. There he quickly ended the disagreement among army doctors over what disease was afflicting the soldiers.

A few of the doctors said the disease was typhoid fever, a "killer" disease for which there was no cure. Most of the army doctors argued that it was malaria, a milder fever that could be treated with quinine. Symptoms of the two diseases were very similar, and a doctor making a

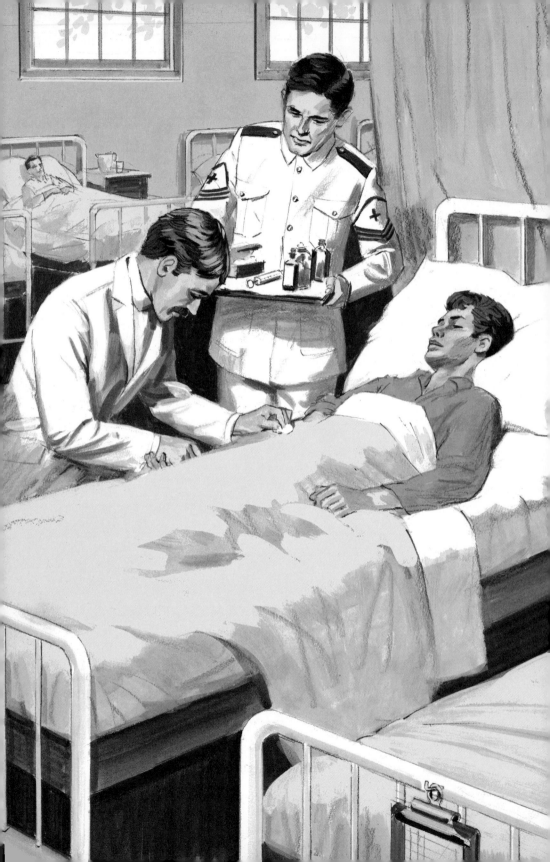

routine examination of a patient might confuse one fever for the other.

But there was no confusion in the laboratory Dr. Reed had installed in the railroad car in which he was traveling. He took blood samples from several of the sick soldiers and made a simple test of each sample. The tests showed no trace of a substance called plasmodium, which always appears in the blood of malaria patients. The soldiers had typhoid fever.

Many camp officials argued that this was impossible. They said that all scientists agreed that Eberth's bacillus, the typhoid bacterium, named for the man who discovered it, is spread only through drinking water. Tests had proved that the water the soldiers drank was pure.

"Then all of the scientists have to be wrong," Dr. Reed replied calmly. "The water is pure indeed, but these soldiers have typhoid fever. The next step is to discover what other methods of transportation are used by Eberth's bacillus."

For two months Dr. Reed made a variety of tests at army camps throughout the South. He examined not only typhoid-fever patients but also the patients' clothing and bedclothing, the dishes from which they ate, and all other items with which the sick came in contact. He found the killer he was searching for and made a new discovery. Typhoid fever can be spread through what Dr. Reed called "comrade infection," or personal contact with a typhoid-fever patient. For the first time victims of the fever were placed in quarantine.

The quarantine helped, but new cases of typhoid continued to appear, and

Dr. Reed kept searching for other ways in which Eberth's bacillus could travel. By the time he reached the army camp at Chickamauga, Tennessee, he had planned his final tests.

The camp was not kept as clean as it should have been. Swarms of flies infested the grounds and buildings. Dr. Reed was suspicious of those flies. He had some soldiers spread lime in the latrines, or outdoor rest rooms. Then he waited in the mess hall for the men to come for their noon meal. Would his theory prove to be correct?

No sooner was the food put on the table than the flies swarmed in through the unscreened windows of the mess hall and settled on the soldiers' plates. Dr. Reed inspected the flies carefully. They were ordinary houseflies, but these particular houseflies had white legs—white from the lime that had been spread in the latrines.

Dr. Reed took samples of the food on which the flies had alighted. When he examined the food samples under his microscope, he found that some contained Eberth's bacillus. The army camps were cleaned up, attempts were made to destroy

the flies, and screens were installed on windows of all buildings. Soon the typhoid epidemic ended. More than 20,000 soldiers had suffered from the disease, and 1,580 of them had died. Dr. Reed returned to Washington and prepared to write a full report of all he had learned about Eberth's bacillus, so that doctors everywhere could help prevent typhoid.

The report had to wait. An epidemic of yellow fever broke out among American soldiers who had been sent to occupy Cuba after the Spanish-American war ended.

"Yellow fever!" Emilie exclaimed with horror. "Lawrence is in Cuba!"

"This is another job for you, Dr. Reed," Dr. Sternberg said, and Walter packed his bags to leave for Cuba. He knew this job would be harder than his work on the typhoid epidemic, because this time he did not know the invisible killer. No one had discovered what bacterium, or other agent, caused the disease. Most medical men agreed that yellow fever was spread by *fomites*, pronounced FOH-mah-tees. That was a general word used to describe the discharges of yellow-fever patients, and also the bedclothing and other articles soiled by the patients.

Dr. Reed had to try to find the killer, and also find a way to destroy it. Emilie could not hide her fears as she said good-bye to Walter. "You know I will worry," she said. "Any disease the soldiers can get, you can get too."

"But I might also find a way to prevent others from having yellow fever," Walter reminded her. "That is why I must go."

8. "Yellow Jack"

Dr. Reed waited patiently at the bedside of a yellow-fever patient in the hospital at Camp Columbia, near Havana, Cuba. His young assistant, Dr. Jesse Lazear, held the open mouth of a test tube against the arm of the patient. A mosquito, trapped inside the tube, finally settled on the patient's arm and began to feed.

In a few days that same mosquito would bite Dr. James Carroll, another of Dr. Reed's assistants. "And a few days after that, Dr. Carroll will have yellow fever," Dr. Lazear said confidently.

"I wish I could believe that," Dr. Reed said, and his voice revealed his discouragement.

For six weeks Dr. Reed and three assistants had worked day and night, searching for the bacterium that caused yellow fever, or "yellow jack," as the soldiers called it. The nickname had come about because of the yellow quarantine flag used to warn people to stay away from a building or ship housing the sick. That flag had been flying over the Camp Columbia hospital since the war ended, as hundreds of soldiers caught the disease.

Dr. Reed and his researchers studied blood samples of patients and tested body tissue from the dead. Fomites from hundreds of patients were examined. The researchers found nothing. That meant that the disease was caused by an "ultra-microscopic" organism—in other words, a virus too tiny to be seen under microscopes of that day.

Even though he could not see the virus, Walter Reed knew that he must discover how it traveled from one person to another. He was now convinced that fomites did not spread the disease. "Doctors and nurses at the hospital do not get yellow jack more often than anyone else, and they are exposed to fomites for hours every day," he said to his assistants.

"Then let's test the mosquito theory," Dr. Lazear said.

For many years Dr. Carlos Finlay, a Cuban, had claimed that yellow jack was spread by a particular mosquito he had named *Culex fasciatus*. Medical men

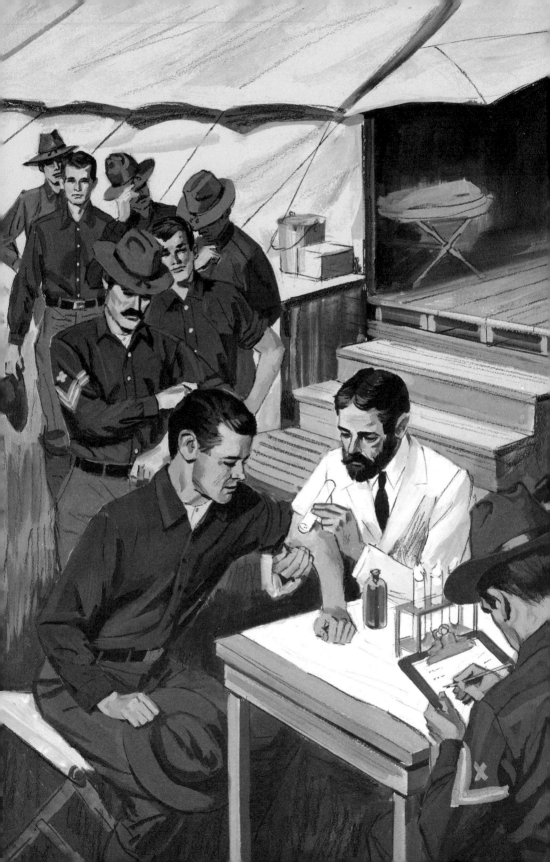

laughed at the notion that a mosquito was the cause of the terrible illness, but Dr. Lazear thought it might be possible. Epidemics always occurred when mosquitoes were thickest.

Dr. Reed agreed to experiment with the mosquitoes. "The worst that can happen is that medical men will laugh at me too," he said. He had to return to Washington to finish his reports on his typhoid-fever studies, but he directed his assistants to go on with the experiments.

For the first three weeks that he was in Washington, Dr. Reed received discouraging reports from his aides in Cuba. Dr. Lazear and seven other volunteers had been bitten by the mosquitoes. Not one had yellow jack. "So the mosquitoes are not the carriers after all," he said to Emilie. "Where do we look now?"

Two weeks later a new report sent Dr. Reed rushing back to Cuba. Dr. Carroll, Dr. Lazear, and one volunteer soldier were all sick with the disease after receiving mosquito bites. By the time Dr. Reed returned to Camp Columbia, Dr. Carroll had recovered, but he was so weak he could scarcely move about. The yellow jack had damaged his heart.

Dr. Lazear did not recover. The eager assistant who had believed in Dr. Finlay's mosquito theory died a few days before Dr. Reed arrived. Sorrowfully, Dr. Reed sat in Dr. Lazear's office, studying the records of the mosquito experiments kept by the careful young scientist. Eight people did not get yellow fever after being bitten by mosquitoes. Three people did. As he compared the cases, Dr. Reed realized that Dr. Lazear's records showed why.

Dr. Lazear, left, and Dr. Carroll, right, both developed yellow fever in experiments with mosquitoes at Camp Columbia, below.

The mosquito must bite a yellow-fever patient within the first three days of that patient's illness in order to pick up the disease. Then the disease must develop inside the body of the mosquito for at least twelve days before the mosquito can pass it on to another person. Even in his excitement, Dr. Reed knew that the medical world would not accept Dr. Lazear's three cases as proof of a new theory. He would have to conduct more experiments.

"Only humans get yellow fever," he said soberly to Dr. Carroll. "No other animal suffers from it. That means we must use 'human guinea pigs' for the experiments."

Only volunteers who knew the risks would be used. But Dr. Reed's heart was heavy as he made plans deliberately to infect other humans with the disease that had killed Dr. Lazear.

9. A Tale of Two Huts

An uncultivated field on a farm about a mile outside Quemados, a Havana suburb, was selected as the place for a camp at which to make the new yellow-fever experiments. Dr. Reed named it Camp Lazear in memory of his friend.

Workmen built two little huts near the center of the field. The buildings were no more than crude shacks because they would be used for only a short time, but they were built according to special plans drawn by Dr. Reed. When the huts were finished the workmen were sent away. Dr. Reed, his assistants, and several men who had volunteered to be "guinea pigs" for the experiments all moved into tents at the edge of the field. No one else was allowed near the camp.

The first hut, called Building Number One, was for the fomites experiment. Building Number One had two tiny windows and a door, all on the same side of the house so that no cross ventilation was possible. The weather was warm in tropical Cuba, but the hut was heated to a temperature of 95 degrees by an oil-burning stove. Tubs of water sat near the stove, to keep the air humid.

Three army cots were the only furnishings. These were covered with bedclothing that had been hideously soiled by yellow-fever patients at the hospital. The odor

This is an artist's conception of Building Number One at Camp Lazear.

was enough to make a person ill. Dr. Reed felt sorry for the three volunteer soldiers who would live in this foul room.

He kept close watch over the men. He was convinced from his own studies that fomites were harmless, even though other doctors believed that fomites spread yellow fever. These volunteers were risking their lives to find out who was right. For twenty nights the three men lived in the hut.

They did not sleep well, but they did not get yellow fever. Dr. Reed was now sure that fomites do not cause yellow fever, but he wanted the world to be as certain as he was. He asked two other volunteers to take their turn living in the filthy hut.

At the same time Dr. Reed started the experiment in Building Number Two. This hut was as healthful as it could be made. Several windows admitted fresh air and sunlight. The floor and walls were scrubbed. Fresh, clean sheets were put on the cots. The room was divided in half by a screen so fine that a mosquito could not squeeze through it. The two halves of the room were exactly alike—in all ways but one.

Two men went into one half of the room. Only one volunteer, a young civilian clerk named John J. Moran, went into the other half, but he had for company fifteen

These brave members of the hospital corps volunteered as ''guinea pigs'' in Dr. Reed's yellow-fever experiments at Camp Lazear.

Culex fasciatus mosquitoes. They had been feeding on yellow-fever patients. Moran was to allow the mosquitoes to bite him as often as they liked. And he was not to slap at them!

On Christmas Day 1900, four days after the experiment started, Dr. Reed visited his "mosquito room" patient. He found young John Moran suffering from a severe headache and a high fever. His skin was a sickly yellow, his eyes were bloodshot, and his bones ached. John had yellow fever. The two men on the other side of the screen remained well.

The men in the fomites hut remained well, too. Dr. Reed had proved the mosquito theory. His friend Major William Crawford Gorgas, who was in charge of the army's sanitation program in Cuba, started at once to destroy every *Culex fasciatus* (now called *Aedes aegypti*) on the island. When the mosquitoes were gone, the yellow-fever epidemic ended. Now everyone was convinced that mosquitoes and yellow fever go together.

Dr. Reed wrote to Emilie to share his success with her. "The prayer that has been mine for twenty years, that I might be permitted in some way or at some time to do something to alleviate human suffering has been granted!" he said.

A few weeks later he returned home to Emilie and Blossom in Washington. Lawrence, still in Cuba, was a second lieutenant and had decided on a career in the army. Susie had returned to her own people, now on a reservation in Oklahoma.

Dr. Reed resumed his job of teaching young men to be good doctors, but he was famous now. Praise for his work came

Blossom Reed and her famous father

from all over the world. He was asked to speak at medical meetings. Several universities gave him honorary degrees. The scholar-adventurer enjoyed his fame for only a short time, however. Less than two years later, Dr. Reed suffered a ruptured appendix and died on November 23, 1902.

He was buried in Arlington National Cemetery. The inscription on the stone over his grave reads, "He gave to man control over that dreadful scourge, yellow fever." The United States government honored the famous doctor not only with a gold medal, but also with a postage stamp bearing his picture. Walter Reed Army Hospital in Washington is named in his memory.

His old friend Major Gorgas, who had helped with the work in Cuba, went to Panama to destroy the mosquitoes and end yellow fever there. With health conditions in the area improved, workmen were then able to build the Panama Canal. Admirers called Major Gorgas a great man for his work in Panama. Gorgas replied, "Not a great man, merely one who is trying to follow in the footsteps of a great man, Walter Reed."

Index

Murfreesboro, N.C., 33, 36, 37

New York City, 29, 30, 32, 34, 38

Panama, 91
Panama Canal, 92

Reed, Annie, 28
Reed, Blossom (daughter), 55, 89, 90 (pic)
Reed, Chris (brother), 7-15, 21, 22, 24, 28, 29, 30, 32, 33, 35
Reed, Emilie Lawrence (wife), 33, 36, 37, 41, 42, 44, 47, 50, 53, 55, 56, 59, 64, 73, 89
Reed, Jim (brother), 13, 16, 21, 22, 28
Reed, Laura (sister), 9, 21, 23
Reed, Lemuel Sutton (father), 8, 9, 14, 16, 17, 20, 21, 22, 28, 29, 30
Reed, Pharaba White (mother), 8, 9, 14, 17, 19-23
Reed, Tom (brother), 13, 16, 21, 22, 28
Reed, Walter
  and bacteriology, 52, 53, 54, 55-58, 61-63
  boyhood of, 7-24
  death of, 91

early years in army, 34-50, 36 (pic)
education of, 21-32
experiments of, 69, 70, 71-73, 75-82, 83-88, 87 (pic)
marriage of, 37
as teacher, 61, 63, 64
tributes to, 91, 92
Reed, Walter Lawrence (son), 47, 50, 55, 65, 73, 89

San Francisco, 38, 39
Sioux Indians, 38, 39, 45
Sitting Bull, 38, 45
Spanish-American War, 64-66
Sternberg, George Miller, 63, 66, 73
Susie (Indian girl), 48, 50, 55, 89

Typhoid fever, 67, 69, 70, 73

Virginia, University of, 21, 22, 24-28

Walter Reed Army Hospital, 91
Wilson, Louis, 61, 62
Willetts Point, 35, 36

Yellow fever, 73-89

94